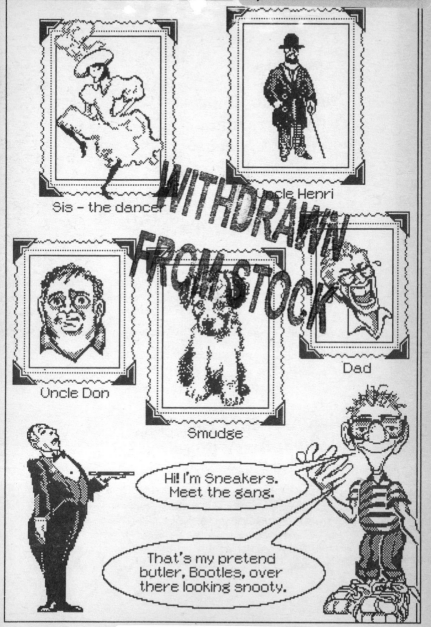

Other Fun titles available in Armada

Crazy - But True!
Crazy Curriculum
Jonathan Clements

The Schoolkids' Joke Book
Compiled by Brough Girling

Holiday Joke Book
Bill Howard

Ghostly Gags
Alan Robertson

Filafun: A Joke Collection
Filafun2: An Activity Collection
Keith Faulkner

Some really funny books here!
Go read them!

SNEAKERS

Edited by

Alan Robertson

most of the computer art

by

Trici Venola

This book is for
Jessie, Dani, Sam, Hannah,
Nessie, Fi, Lorna, Jayne,
Emma, Katy, Rachel
and Lucy.
I love them all!

ARMADA

First published in Armada in 1989

Armada is an imprint of the Children's Division,
part of the Collins Publishing Group,
8 Grafton Street, London W1X 3LA

Printed and bound in Great Britain by
William Collins Sons & Co. Ltd, Glasgow

My
Survival
Guide
To
Food,
Eating Out
and
The High Life.

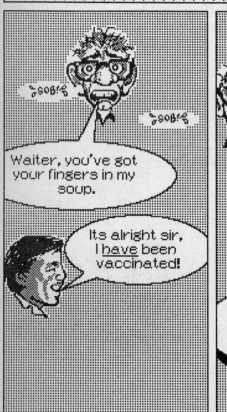

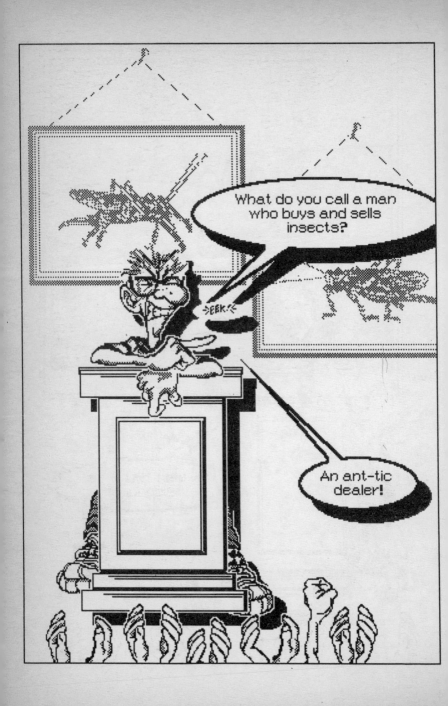

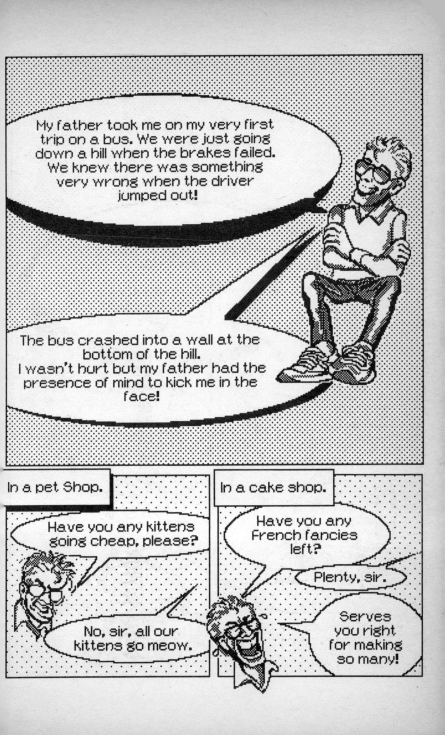

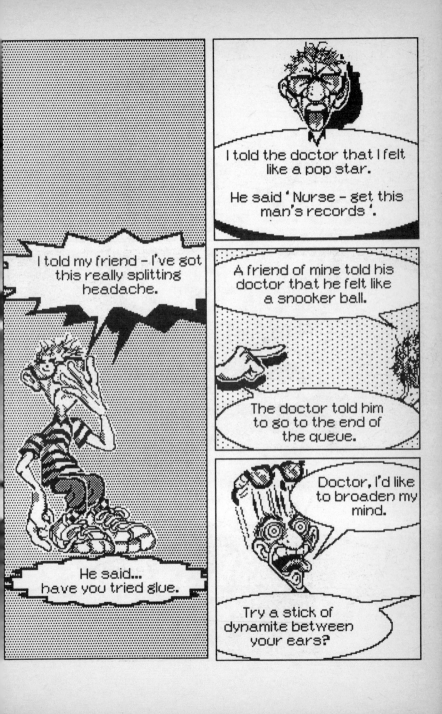

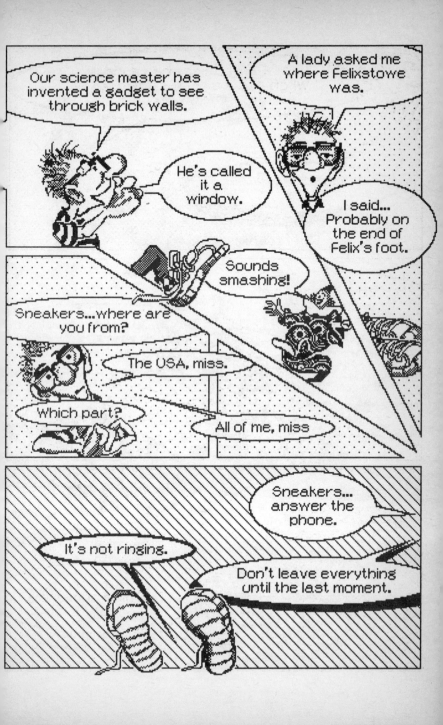

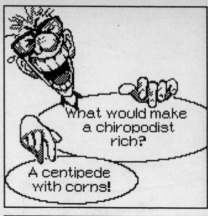

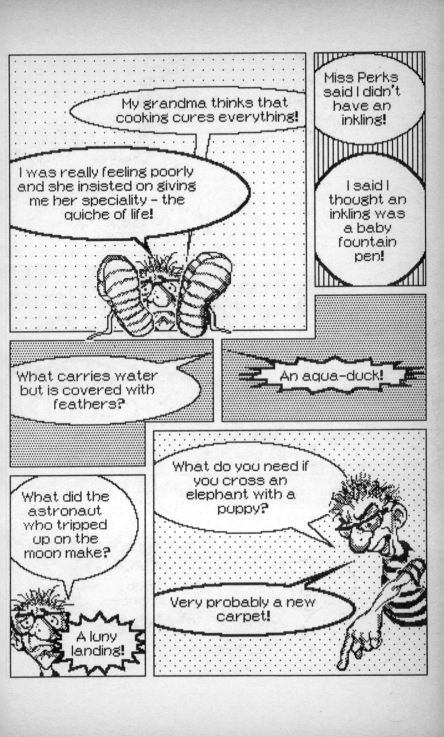

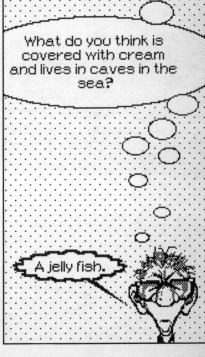

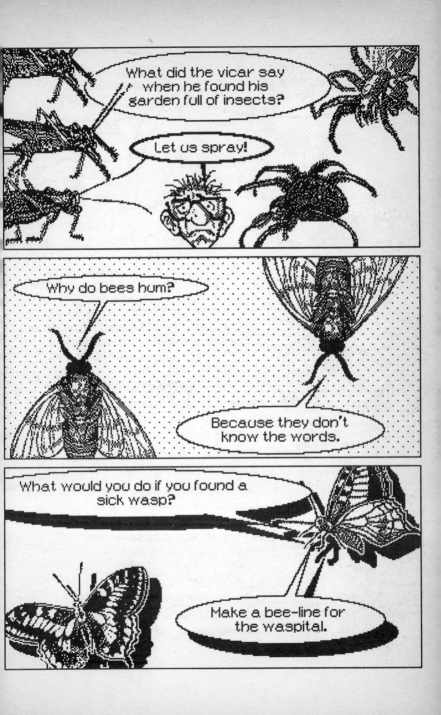

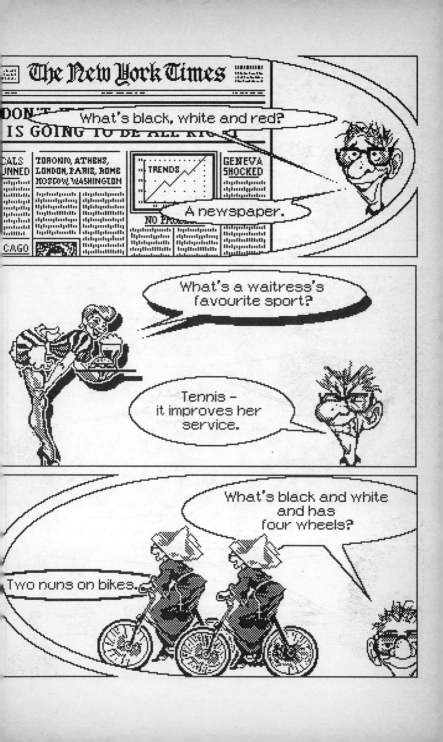

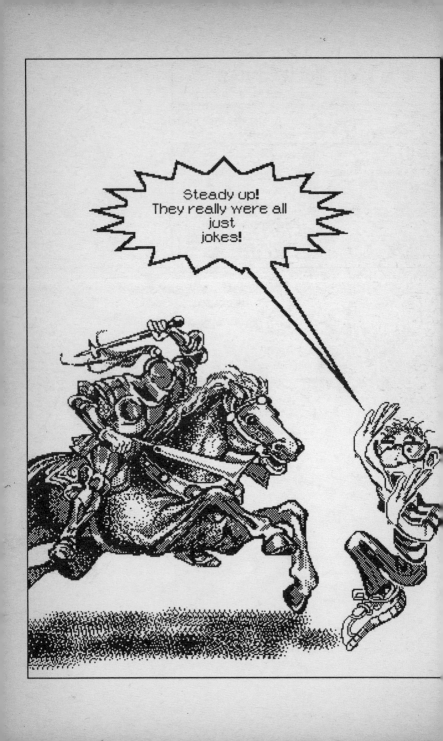